THE WILDEST
ANIMAL ENCOUNTERS IN THE
WILDEST PLACES

THE WILDEST ANIMAL ENCOUNTERS
IN THE WILDEST PLACES

Book cover and interior layout design:
Shabbir Hussain

At Animals Around The Globe we see experiences with animals as a way to strengthen our weakened bond with nature. We believe in a world where humans and animals can live next to each other in peace and harmony.

The founders: Chris and Jan

THE WILDEST ANIMAL ENCOUNTERS IN THE WILDEST PLACES

Written by: Natasha Weber

Jan is the co-founder of Animals Around The Globe. As a little kid, he fell in love with nature, wildlife, and animals. Living in the USA, South Africa, and Germany allowed him to discover the world's wildlife. His favorite animals are Mountain Gorillas, Siberian Tigers, and Great White Sharks. With his wife, Henrieke, he loves to go for game drives in Kruger National Park or dive in the Great Barrier Reef. He holds a PADI Open Water Certificate and a Master of Science in Economics.

Chris is the other co-founder of Animals Around The Globe. Already at a young age, he started to explore wildlife with his family. His wife, Natasha, and him are following this passion and still seek out wild places with wild animals to this date. His favorite locations to see animals are: The Azores, Yosemite National Park & Yellowstone National Park as well as Africa and the Maldives. He has lived in the USA, South Africa, Ireland, Germany, and France which enabled him to get familiar with local wildlife around the globe. He is also a PADI certified diver and holds a Master in Business Administration.

Hello and welcome to our first book from Animals Around the Globe. If you love learning about animals and where you can experience once-in-a-lifetime animal encounters, you have come to the right place.

In this book edition, we are going to go into detail about the wildest animal encounters in the wildest places on Planet Earth. Have you ever thought about what it's like to stand next to mountain gorillas or dive with tiger sharks?

Well, look no further, for we have all of the information on the best spots to see, feel and experience wonderful wildlife! It doesn't matter if you haven't even thought about which animal encounters exist or which ones you may want to experience someday. We are hoping with this guide that you will be inspired to dream beyond the limits of the variety of amazing animal encounters and destinations that exist on beautiful planet Earth.

Read on to learn more, and if you don't have time to read through the whole book, be sure to go to the contents page below to skip to the section of your choice.

"If we can teach people about wildlife, they will be touched. Share my wildlife with me. Because humans want to save things that they love."

~Steve Irwin

CONTENTS

TOP **9** MOST EXCITING WILDLIFE ENCOUNTERS

1 Swimming with Orcas

Orcas are one of the most intelligent and prominent species of toothed oceanic dolphins. It is also the largest member of this family and is recognizable by its black-and-white patterned body. Orcas can be found in all of the world's oceans, from the Arctic region to more tropical seas.

One of the best places to swim with Orcas is wintery northern Norway, where large quantities of herring gather which attract the orcas. What is even more fascinating is that hundreds and even thousands of whales gather here to hunt. But, if you are interested in experiencing this encounter, be aware that there poses a number of challenges including the cold air and water temperatures, snow, ice, little daylight, and swell in the water. Top tip: the cold and crystal clear fjord waters are perfect for observing orca pods. Those who have been so lucky to experience this encounter have said that many mammals have been seen, sometimes in pods of 200 or more.

If you want to know more about the details as to when is the best time to go to Norway for this encounter, read about it in the section of this book titled "Top Winter Wildlife Encounters."

2 Diving with Tiger Sharks

The tiger shark is the fourth largest shark in the world after the whale, basking, and great white sharks. It can grow to five meters long and weighs over 1,000 kilograms. It is a mainly nocturnal and solitary animal that has the widest amount of food out of all the sharks, snacking on fish, seals, sea snakes, and even other smaller sharks. Usually, the populations of tiger sharks can be mainly concentrated in tropical waters, especially around the central Pacific islands.

You can experience and dive with tiger sharks in a few different locations. The best of these are Tiger Beach, Bahamas, Fuvah Mulah, Maldives, and Beqa Island in Fiji. If you are keen to see which dive schools and centers offer these experiences, feel free to skip to the section of this book titled "Top Water Wildlife Encounters."

For some general inspiration, we wanted to teach you some fun facts about tiger sharks. They are one of the largest shark species, with the possibility of growing up to 18 feet (5.5 m) long and 2,000 pounds (900kg). Also, tiger sharks are named for their gray vertical stripes or spots covering the sides of their bodies. We are sure that if you weren't already, these creatures have fascinated you!

3 Safari Drive with Brown **Bears**

Fun fact! They are mainly known as Brown Bears in Europe, but in North America, they are known as Grizzly Bears - named after their gray fur coat. It is one of the largest types of bears, rivaled in size only by the polar beach which is slightly bigger on average. The brown bear is the most variable in size of modern bears as the typical size depends on which population it is from.

You may be wondering where you can see brown bears, and you may be guessing correctly! They are found in forests and mountains across Europe, Asia, and North America. In fact, the world's largest brown bears are located in the coastal regions of Alaska and British Columbia - on islands such as Kodiak.

If you live in Europe or are interested in where to travel to in Europe and are a brown bear enthusiast, you can also find them in Northern Finland as well as in Greece! If you would like to learn more about where you can see brown bears, check out our section later in this book titled "Top Summer Wildlife Encounters."

4 Canoe Safari with **Hippos**

From water animals to bears and now to canoe safaris with hippos - how amazing is the wildlife that exists in our world? We should never take it for granted.

Hippos are large semi-aquatic mammals with a sizable barrel-shaped body, short legs, a short tail, and an enormous head! They have grayish to muddy-brown skin, which fades to a pale pink color underneath. They are considered the second largest land animal on Earth (the first place goes to the elephant!).

Fun fact: the closest living relatives of the hippo family are cetaceans (whales and dolphins etc) which came from 55 million years ago.

You can find hippos lurking around rivers, lakes, and mangrove swamps. They tend to walk underwater rather than swim. They can stay underwater for 5-8 minutes, and birth is also usually underwater where the young animals can swim immediately.

Hippos can be found today in Sub-Saharan Africa. They are rare in Western Africa and it is estimated that only 130,000 specimens live in freedom.

5 Snorkel with **Manatees** and **Dugongs**

Manatees are large, fully aquatic, primarily herbivorous marine mammals, sometimes known as sea cows. The dugong is a medium-sized marine mammal. It is one of four living species of the order Sirenia, including three manatees species. Dugongs are related to manatees and are similar in appearance and behavior– though the dugong's tail is fluked like a whale's. Both are related to the elephant, although the giant land animal is not similar in appearance or behavior.

You can find dugongs in the warm coastal waters from the Western Pacific Ocean to the Eastern coast of Africa, usually in protected shallow bays. Manatees live in the shallow waters of marine coastal areas and freshwater habitats. They can also be found in the warm water of tropical regions only. To read in more detail about where exactly you can snorkel with them and what to expect, skip to section "Top Water Wildlife Encounters."

6 Cuddle with Koala Bears

Surely, everyone must love koala bears. They are only found in one place in the world, Australia, due to their staple diet of Eucalyptus leaves which they can eat 2.5 pounds of food a day. The koala hops from tree to tree and climbs to get the leaves.

In Australia, koalas inhabit the mainland and see islands on the eastern and southeastern coasts. Areas of these are dependent on the availability of trees and the fertility of the soil in the area.

Specifically, you are more likely to see a koala if you visit Raymond Island VIC, Kennett River, VIC, Cape Otway, VIC, Port Stephens NSW, or Kangaroo Island, SA. Be sure to support NGOs and sanctuaries that support koala bear protection and rehabilitation. A couple of great resources that we recommend looking into, include WWF Australia and koalahospital.com which helps to rescue and treat sick and injured koalas and release them back to their homes where possible.

7 Boating with **Whales** and **Dolphins**

People use the term dolphin, porpoise, and whale to describe marine mammals from the order Cetacean. Whales (*Cetaceans*) are divided into two group's baleen whales (*Mysticeti*) and toothed whales (*Odontoceti*). The main difference is that baleen whales have baleen and two blowholes, while toothed whales have teeth and one blowhole.

Dolphins are toothed whales; the largest dolphin is the Orca (generally mistaken for a whale due to its name, killer whale). A related family to dolphins is Porpoises. Often, people confuse dolphins and porpoises, but there are differences to look out e.g. their faces, teeth, fins, and figures. Dolphins tend to have prominent, elongated snouts & cone-shaped teeth, while porpoises have smaller mouths and spade-shaped teeth. The dolphin's hooked or curved dorsal fin differs from the porpoise's triangular dorsal fin.

To learn more about where are the best places to go boating to see these fascinating animals, skip to the section of this book titled, "Top Water Wildlife Encounters."

8 Bush Safari Tour aside/hot air balloon above **wildebeest** migration

Another exciting wildlife encounter occurs on the continent of Africa. The wildebeest migration is one of the largest migrations on Earth. They are joined by around 400,000 antelopes and 200,000 zebras in a spectacular 3000 km journey that is a privilege to witness. On a yearly occasion, a huge number of different animals make their way across the Serengeti to the Masai Mara. Imagine experiencing such a journey of many animals.

Generally speaking, the best time to see the Great Migration is from July to October, though this can change slightly depending on factors beyond human control.

If you want to learn more about the different tour options available for experiencing this once-in-a-lifetime migration, read more in the section of this book titled: "Top 6 Summer Wildlife Encounters."

15

9 Watch **wolves** and other animals in Germany

There is no doubt that Germany is a great place to visit, but have you ever considered the wildlife that resides in the countryside and cities of Germany? It is often overlooked by many! For more than a century, wolves were extinct in Germany. In recent years, however, especially since the country's reunification in 1990, the animals have been reintroduced and are slowly making a comeback. They are especially prevalent in Eastern Germany since many have crossed the border with Poland.

TOP **6** WILDLIFE DESTINATIONS IN AFRICA

1 Queen Elizabeth **National Park**, Uganda

The first incredible wildlife destination that we recommend is in Uganda.

Uganda's most famous safari site is the country's second-largest and most biodiverse park. The park, which is located in western Uganda near the Rwenzori Mountains, encompasses a diverse range of landscapes,

including wetlands, swamps, crater lakes, tropical forests, woodland, and open savannah, and supports a diverse range of wildlife, including 95 mammal species and over 600 bird species.

Highlights of local wildlife wonders include easily observed elephants and buffalo, Ugandan kob, sitatunga, big forest hog, and topi – with tree-climbing lions in the park's south section topping the list. You can go on boat cruises to witness hippos and crocodiles in addition to wildlife drives on the open savannah. You can also hike through the rainforest to find chimpanzees.

2 Okavango Delta, Botswana

Another beautiful wildlife destination to visit is situated in Botswana in Southern Africa. What makes it truly special is that it is one of the world's largest inland deltas. The Okavango River, unlike most river deltas, flows onto open land, flooding the savanna and forming a unique and ever-changing inland delta.

The Okavango Delta is regarded as one of the most beautiful wilderness locations on the planet. You can see many different types of wildlife including the African Bush Elephant, Hippopotamus as well as Cheetahs and Leopards.

In the Okavango Delta, lions have adapted to their water habitat and thrive. Don't be startled if you see a lion swimming slowly closer to its prey. A lion pride can have anything from three to thirty members; the more, the better. These large cats are pretty friendly. If you are interested in experiencing and exploring the Okavango Delta, the best time to go is between June and August and September to October. Having said that, due to a combination of wetlands and abundant resident safari, the Okavango Delta is a great option for an all year round safari experience.

3 Sabi Sands Park, South Africa

Sabi Sands Park is situated adjacent to Kruger National Park. The Sabi Sands benefits from a wide diversity of species found in one of the most incredible wildlife locations on the African continent. It is mainly well known for leopard sightings, given there are no boundary walls between it and Kruger Park.

The Big Five, as well as additional animals. The Big Five are well-known in the Sabi Sands (Lion, Leopard, Elephant, Buffalo, and Rhino). It was in the Sabi Sands when the Big Five concept was reborn as a classic safari term. If you can imagine the spectacular sight of the Sabi Sands leopards, normally elusive, becoming habituated to safari vehicles, allowing visitors incredible photography opportunities and lifetime memories.

4 Etosha National Park, Namibia

Etosha National Park is the only one of its kind in Africa. The park's major feature is a massive salt pan that can be viewed from space. Yet, because so much wildlife congregates around the waterholes, game sightings are nearly inevitable.

At the same time, Etosha National Park is one of Namibia's and Southern Africa's most accessible wildlife reserves. Etosha National Park is one of Africa's most excellent savannah conservation areas, including elephants, black and white rhinoceros, lions, leopards, cheetahs, enormous herds of springbok, zebra, wildebeest, giraffes, and a plethora of other intriguing animals, big and little.

5 Maasai Mara
National Reserve

The Masai Mara National Reserve is located in the southeast of Kenya. The northern section of the Serengeti Ecosystem spans 25,000 square kilometers and comprises the National Serengeti Park and the Ngorongoro Conservation Area, in addition to the Masai Mara in Kenya.

The Maasai Mara is one of Africa's most well-known and vital wildlife conservation and wilderness areas, known for its remarkable lion, African leopard, cheetah, and African bush elephant populations. The Maasai Mara is also Kenya's isolated protected area with an indigenous black rhino population undisturbed by translocations. It can host one of Africa's largest populations due to its size.

6 The Ngorongoro Crater, Tanzania

Ngorongoro, the world's largest intact volcanic caldera and home to Africa's highest population of big game, is undoubtedly the most famous crater. These volcanic craters provide a magnificent backdrop to some of Africa's most fertile and abundant grazing lands.

The Ngorongoro Crater is home to an extraordinary variety of species, including all five members of the Big Five. Hippopotamus, zebras, crocodiles, antelope, leopards, cheetahs, and lions are all found here. Approximately 25,000 large animals are thought to live within this natural and enclosed sanctuary.

TOP **6** WILDLIFE DESTINATIONS IN SOUTH AMERICA

Whilst you were dreaming of a safari experience in one of the many beautiful destinations that exist on the African continent, we wanted to bring your attention towards the incredibly unique wildlife experiences that exist in South America. From the lush, thick ecosystems in the Amazon Rainforest to the melting point of marine species in the Galapagos, South America has everything for those seeking a wildlife adventure. Read on to find out more.

1 Canaima National Park, Venezuela

Canaima National Park is a three million-hectare park near the Guyana-Brazil border in south-eastern Venezuela. Table mountain (tepui) formations cover roughly 65% of the park. You can see and experience many different varieties of animals, including cougars, two-toed sloths, toucans, and opossums.

There are many waterfalls and lagoons that can be visited from the Canaima camp, but probably the most famous one is Angel Falls which can be reached via Canaima National Park. It sits on a UNESCO World Heritage Site and the World's Highest Waterfall, according to UNESCO.

The flat-topped table mountain (tepui) formations of Canaima National Park in southeast Venezuela are distinctive and hold deep cultural significance to the Pemon communities of Venezuela. Tepuis are a unique biotic ecosystem with an essential evolutionary story about the earth's evolution.

2 Galapagos Islands, Ecuador

Consisting of 19 islands and an adjacent marine reserve, the Galapagos Islands are located 1000 km from the South American continent in the Pacific Ocean and have been named a unique "living museum and showcase of evolution."

The Galápagos Islands are a 'melting pot' of marine species because they are located at the confluence of three ocean currents. Seismic and volcanic activity are still active, reflecting the processes that created the islands. Following his visit in 1835, these processes, together with the islands' splendid isolation, led to the formation of unusual animal life, including the land iguana, giant tortoise, and various finches, which inspired Charles Darwin's theory of evolution by natural selection.

One of the most beautifully diverse and rich areas of marine life in the world, the best time of the year to visit the Galapagos Islands is from December to May due to the warm season and warmer and clearer ocean conditions for snorkeling and diving.

3 The **Amazon Basin**, Brazil

The Amazon Rainforest is a tropical rainforest that covers most of the Amazon basin of South America. It is a crucial rainforest that manages the global oxygen and carbon cycles. In fact, it produces about 6% of the world's oxygen and has long been assumed to operate as a carbon sink.

This basin encompasses 7,000,000 km2 (2,700,000 sq mi), of which 5,500,000 km2 (2,100,000 sq mi) are covered by the rainforest. Also, the Amazon is home to sloths, black spider monkeys, and poison dart frogs as well as one of Earth's final refuges for jaguars, harpy eagles, and pink river dolphins. Nine countries share the Amazon Basin, and there are many tours and other experiences that can be made so that you too can book your perfect wildlife experience here.

4 The **Colca** **Canyon,** Peru

Colca Canyon is situated in Southern Peru and lies at 2,110 meters (6,922 feet) above sea level. It is one of the deepest canyons in the world and has a length of around 70km (43 miles). Whilst trekking in the Colca Canyon, you can see that there are still some people who inhabit the Canyon (the Collagua and the Cabana cultures). The local people maintain their traditions within this area.

Something that is pretty spectacular to view within the Colca Canyon are the condors. Specifically, it is home to the Andean condor. The condors can be seen at close range as they fly past the canyon walls. The Andean Condor has a wingspan of around 2.1 - 2.7 meters (7-9 ft) and is sometimes referred to as the 'Eternity Bird" as the bird epitomizes a long life. If you want to experience this beautiful bird in its true habitat, then be sure to check out 'Cruz del Condor' which is a popular stop to view them.

5 Tayrona National Park

Tayrona National Park is situated in the Colombian northern Caribbean region, about 34 km (21 miles) away from the city of Santa Marta. This national park features a variety of climates including a mountain climate and covers around 30 sq km (12 sq miles) of maritime area in the Caribbean sea and then around 150 sq km (58 sq miles) of land.

In the National Park, it is home to three
species of monkeys: capuchins, endangered cotton-top
tamarins, and red howlers. If you are interested in experiencing
this wildlife up and close, then your best chance is to hike the
park's quieter trails early in the morning or at dusk.

Other interesting wildlife to experience here includes one of the park's 300 species of birds which
include the montane solitary eagle, black-backed antshrike and military macaw. There are 31 species
of reptiles, 15 species of amphibians and 401 species of sea and river fish - therefore a true variety of
spectacular biodiversity will be on show at the Tayrona National Park.

6 Amboró National Park

Amboro National Park is situated in central Bolivia with many different species of birds, and mammalian species including the puma, but something more unique about this place is the opportunity to see and experience the rare spectacled bear. The national park covers an area of 4,425 km² or (1,709 sq miles) and is situated adjacent to the Carrasco National Park, where together they form a larger biodiversity unit.

Amboro National Park is ideal for those looking to escape towards a relaxing jungle paradise to connect deeper with nature. The best time to visit Amboro is in the dry season as with the cooler weather, the trails are less muddy with fewer mosquitos. Given the sheer variety of wildlife available to see here, it's a pretty spectacular experience, and due to difficult terrain, much of the national park hasn't been botanically surveyed which means that it's highly likely that there exist more plant and animal species here.

TOP **6** WILDLIFE DESTINATIONS IN THE UNITED STATES

Welcome to the top 6 wildlife destinations to experience in the United States. The third most populous country in the world, the United States, which is situated in North America includes most climate and geographic types. From the coastal plains of the Atlantic to the flat, fertile prairie of the Great Plains, to the Rocky Mountains out West, and volcanoes that lie in Hawaii and Yellowstone. It's clear that for wildlife and nature lovers, the United States has a strong variety of places to see and wildlife to encounter. If you are intrigued to learn more, read ahead.

1 Yellowstone National Park

Yellowstone National Park is located in the western United States, largely in the northwest corner of Wyoming and extending into Montana and Idaho. It was the world's first national park and is one of America's most famous. Yellowstone is home to grizzly and black bears, hundreds of wild bison, wolf packs, massive waterfalls, and the world's most significant concentration of active geysers.

Yellowstone has two types of bears: grizzly bears and black bears. Only the Greater Yellowstone Ecosystem and northwest Montana have considerable grizzly bear populations south of the Canadian border. Around Yellowstone Lake, Fishing Bridge, Hayden and Lamar valleys, Swan Lake Flats, and the East Entrance are the best viewing places. The Bison has been made famous as the USA's official state mammal and is also known as a buffalo, the bison. The American bison has a long and varied history in the United States. Nearly 30 million bison roamed the Great Plains 150 years ago. Lamar Valley is undoubtedly the best spot in Yellowstone to watch wildlife. The grasslands that cover this valley, carved by glaciers and fed by the Lamar River, are easily accessible on Highway 212 and attract the park's largest land species, such as the bison, elk, moose, and bears.

2 Wind Cave National Park

Situated in South Dakota and established in 1912, Wind Cave is one of the earliest reservations to be set aside for animal conservation. The park is perhaps best known for its underground maze filled with intricate box work [which are rare honeycomb-like calcite formations).

On the plains of Wind Cave, animal sightings will require a little more patience and perseverance. But the payoff includes some of the rarest animal species you can imagine. A particular one of note is the pronghorn antelope [the second fastest land animal], which was especially reintroduced into this region of South Dakota in an attempt at wildlife conservation.

In addition, you are likely to encounter land animals such as the desert cottontail, bison, big-eared bats, elks, and more! There exists plentiful birdlife including kingbirds, western tanagers, falcons, and hawks. If you are visiting Wind Cave, the open prairie near the south entrance of the park is the best place to spot pronghorn antelopes.

3 Grand Teton National Park

Located in Wyoming and situated just 30 miles south of Yellowstone park, Grand Teton is perhaps one of the few temperate ecosystems left on the planet. Grand Teton encompasses varying habitats. From imposing 70,000 feet high Teton peaks to low-lying plains, wetlands, and mountain meadows, this diversity of habitats draws in a large variety of wildlife. It also features probably one of the most photographed wildlife spots; the iconic Oxbow Bend.

Whatever your interests, this park has a lot to offer. The mountains alone are a thing of imagination, and you can explore over 200 miles of trails around them. Likewise, the serene rivers such as the Buffalo Fork, Gros Ventre, Pacific Creek, Cascade Creek, and the famous Snake River.

When it comes to teeming wildlife, you can be sure to spot bison, bighorn sheep, yellow-bellied marmot, river otters, pronghorn antelopes, coyotes, and black bears! Keep your eyes out and you will certainly see some bald eagles flying overhead. You can take in the scenery of Grand Teton by kayaking or canoeing through its abundant rivers, hiking, or driving through the paved roads along the mountains. In particular, the boat rides offer a great vantage point for up-close observation. What are you waiting for? For wildlife enthusiasts, Grand Teton surely has it all!

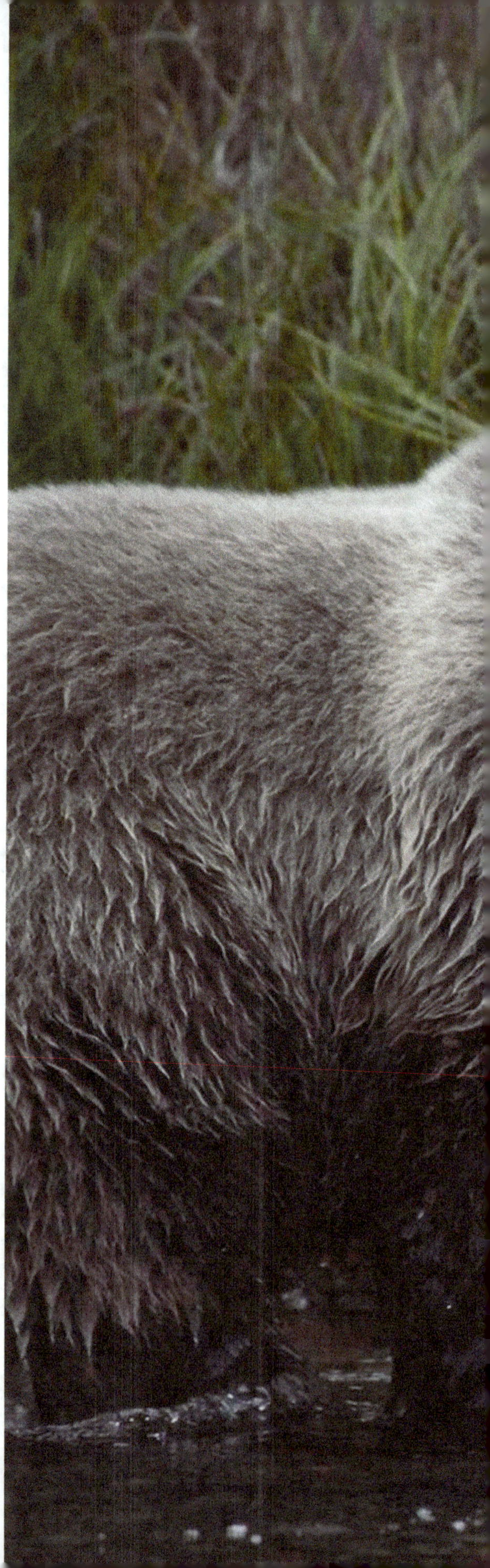

4 Katmai National Park

Located in the state of Alaska, if you love bears, Katmai National Park is arguably the best wildlife conservation reserve for bear-watching. Perhaps you've seen any documentary footage of brown bears fishing for salmon near a waterfall? Almost certainly, that shot was taken within Alaska's Katmai National Park by the filmmakers.

With roughly 2,200 bears coming to this place home, Katmai is a sensational park to have a one-of-a-kind experience of bear-watching away from crowds of people. The park only has five miles of designated hiking trails and you can even explore beyond the trails as you, please.

As no roads from the outside lead directly into Katmai, you would need to take a flight to the nearest town of King Salmon and then a 45-minute water taxi or float plane to get to your destination. But the remoteness is a part of the beauty of this experience.

During the late summer months, you can see grizzly bears at the riverbanks. They're usually eating up their weight in salmon in preparation for the long winter. There is even a celebration for this by the National Park Service known as Fat Bear Week. If you intend on journeying into the wilderness of Katmai, there is a great chance you will stumble across dozens of grizzly bears in close encounters.

5 Glacier National Park

Nicknamed the "Crown of the North American Continent," this all-encompassing Wildlife Conservation Park borders Canada's Waterton Lakes National Park. Together, they are known as the Waterton-Glacier International Peace Park, the first of its kind in the world.

From towering snow-capped peaks and luxuriant valleys to animated waterfalls, lakes, and pristine forests, a trip to Glacier National Park gives you the feel of going back in time to when America's wilderness was still pristine and largely untouched. With regard to wildlife, Glacier National Park houses one of the highest grizzly bear populations in the lower 48 states, as well as herds of elks [about 7,300 of them], the surefooted mountain goat [the park's official mascot], mountain lions, gray wolves, black bear, moose and more! In addition are 270 species of birds, including the native northern American bald eagle and the golden eagle.

If you have ever desired close encounters with grizzlies, Glacier Park is the reserve for you. With over 700 miles of trails to explore, you can expect a breath-taking array of flora and fauna.

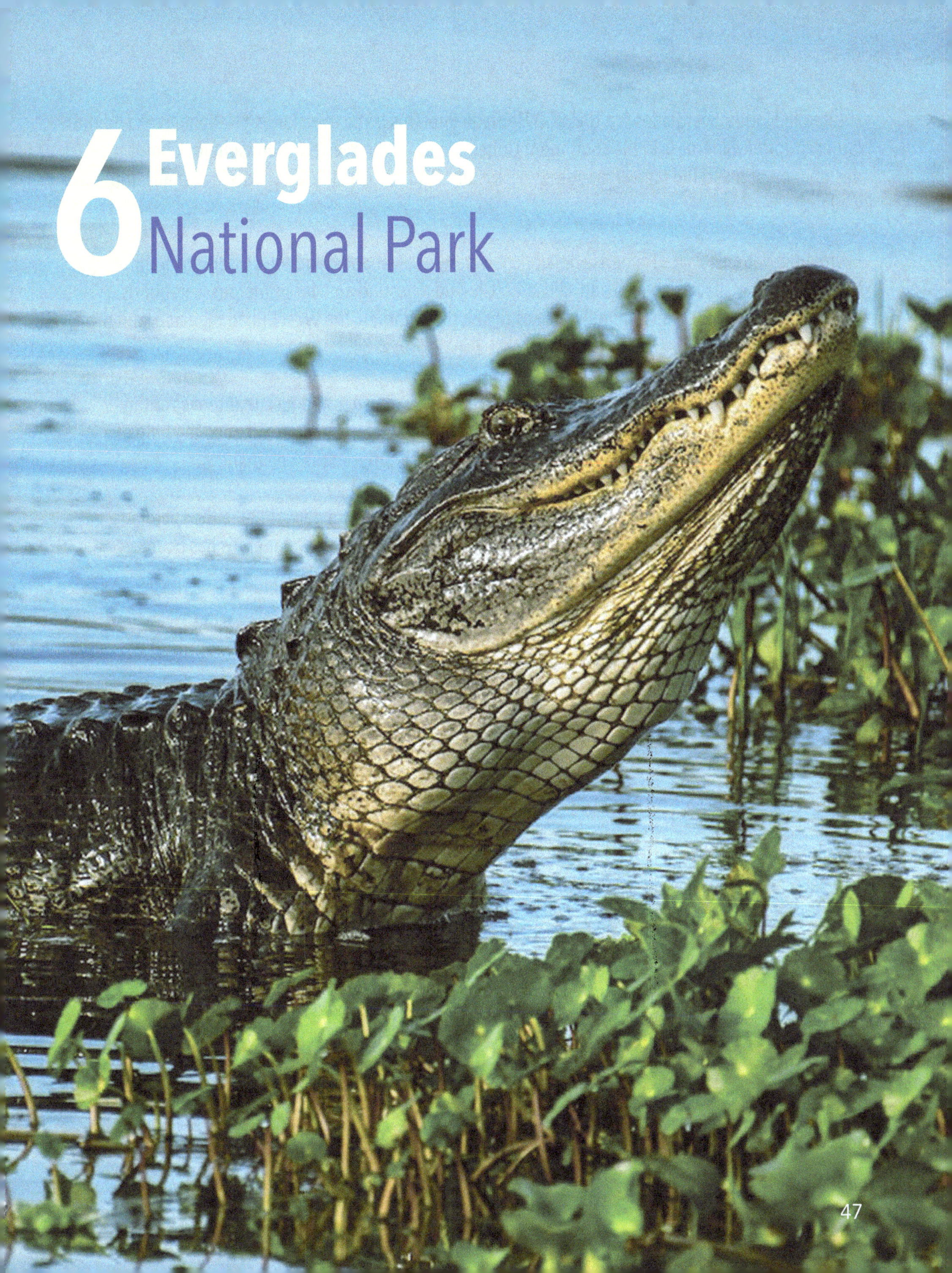
6 Everglades
National Park

Located in Florida, Everglades is a UNESCO Heritage Site. This is the third-largest National Park and the largest tropical wilderness in the contingent United States. In the Western Hemisphere, it holds the designation of being the largest mangrove ecosystem. And it is considered an internationally important wetland.

Everglades National Park's immense network of waterways, wetlands, and forests serve as a climacteric habitat for many species of fresh and saltwater fish. And a nesting area for numerous water birds. Here, you'll find endangered animals such as the Florida panther, the West Indian manatee, and the American crocodile.

Additionally, with over 200,000 of them living in the grassy marshes and lush mangroves of the Everglades, the American alligator is by far the main attraction of the park. You'll need the help of a guide to marshal the meandering channels and find these reptiles in their element.

Airboat touring, canoeing, and kayaking are the activities you can look forward to in the Everglades. These touring rides are the most efficient way to spot wildlife in this ecosystem. This has been a testament to the fantastic effects of wildlife conservation.

TOP **6** WINTER WILDLIFE ENCOUNTERS

1 Swimming with Orcas

You may have already read about swimming with Orcas in Norway in the first section of this book titled "Top 9 Most Exciting Wildlife Encounters." If you are interested in learning more about when to do, which tours are offered and more, you are in the right place in our book.

There are several tours offering the option to do 3 day and 6 day orca expedition trips. One example is Strømsholmen Seasportcenter. The best time of the year to expect orcas is every year from the end of October to January, there is the largest gathering of orcas in far north Norway due to a large amount of herring. In this particular tour, they follow the orcas closely to watch them play and observe their actions. When it is possible to do so, people can go into the water and swim with them.

Also, Orcas Norway is offering the chance to swim or snorkel with these fascinating animals with the season running through the winter into January. So, if you would like to be a part of this once-in-a-lifetime experience, we hope you have been even more inspired!

2 Snowmobiling with Bisons

West Yellowstone is often dubbed as the "Snowmobiling capital of the world," but in the wintery months, as bears are hibernating, you can get onto a snowmobile and drive through the miles of the beauty of this national park.

As you are driving around the park and taking in the beauty, you may get the chance to drive by bison herds. They use the trails to get around in the winter to conserve their energy as there is less food available to them. Though, always be attentive to driving the snowmobile as it is bison territory. Some examples of tours that offer snowmobiles in Jackson Hole, Wyoming are Teton Tour Company, Old Faithful Snowmobile Tours and Scenic Safaris Snowmobile Adventures.

3 Whale watching

At the beginning of each year, humpback whales make their annual migration from Alaska to Hawaii and it's the perfect time for wildlife enthusiasts to witness their beauty from a respectful distance. You can experience this in Maui in Hawaii. Whether you decide to experience this from a larger boat or a smaller raft, you will not only see one of the world's most incredible creatures, but also experience stunning nature and scenery as a backdrop.

A number of companies in Hawaii offer these tours, these include PacWhale Eco-Adventures - Whale Watch Sail, Ultimate Whale Watch & Snorkel – Maui Whale Watching, and Trilogy – Kaanapali Whale Watch. The first of these offers a two-hour tour on a catamaran to spot the humpback whales off the coast of Maui. The second tour is also two hours and includes talks by the onboard marine naturalist. The third tour is on a luxury catamaran featuring a whale naturalist who shares more information about the whales. Whichever way you decide to go with your tour, you can't go wrong, and this will surely be an experience of a lifetime.

4 Encounter Elk Herds

If you decide to take a snowmobile and see some bison on your ride, you may also decide to try to encounter some elk herds as well! Elk are one of the largest members of the deer family.

In multiple areas across the western United States, you will see these social animals gathering together and meandering across their territory. For instance: in the Grand Teton National Park, you can opt in for a horse-drawn sleigh ride through the refuge for an up-close view as well as an informative guide about the thousands of elk herds that exist there.

5 Chilling with Penguins

Have you ever wondered what Antarctica is like? The most remote area of our Earth which spends half of the year in the dark and cold. But, did you know that six of the world's seventeen penguin species can be found here? If you are down for an adventure to see them, there are tour guides and flights that can set you up so that you have a magical time.

The best time to see penguins in Antarctica is between December and February as this is when they are ready to breed and raise chicks. Not only can you experience this unique animal in Antarctica, but also, you can check out the vastness and beauty of our Southernmost continent.

6 Moose migration

Every year, the 'Great Moose Migration" happens in Northern Sweden. The Swedish moose walk down the same path to get to their summer grazing areas. Did you know that they have been traveling this exact journey for around 9,000 years.

There are multiple local guides who are offering the option to experience these majestic animals on their journey.

For instance: Junsele Wilderness offers visitors the chance to see them as their WIlderness Cabins are just 15 minutes away from this wildlife event. Also, Wild Sweden offers a Moose Safari which takes place in the evening for about 5 hours. Whatever you decide to do, if you can experience this animal event, it's a spectacle you'll never forget.

TOP **6** SUMMER WILDLIFE ENCOUNTERS

1 Safari Drive with
Brown Bears

You may be here because you have read about the possibilities to see brown bears around the world in the first section of this book titled "Top 9 most exciting wildlife encounters." It's true that there are many places around the world where you can see them, including in Alaska and British Columbia, as well as Yellowstone National Park. What you may not know is that there are 450 brown bears in Greece. Callisto, a conservation NGO working in the Pindos Mountains is trying to preserve their habitat.

If you want to know where to see brown bears in Alaska, from July through to early September, the bears appear near the mouth of rivers and smaller streams to eat salmon. You are more likely to see the bears when they are actively searching for food, at dawn or at dusk. There are a number of areas where you can see the grizzly bears, for instance at Sitka and Skagway. In other areas of the world, since bears hibernate in the winter, you could see them if you are looking through the Northern hemisphere during the summer months.

2 Safari in
Sri Lanka

Sri Lanka is home to many different species of animals and is filled with a variety of biodiversity, from rainforests, and mountains to beaches and safaris. The best time of year to go on a wildlife adventure here is the inter-monsoon season from July to September. In particular, Yala National Park, which is home to one of the greatest concentrations of leopards in the world. Not only can you see a leopard on your safari, but also, you can get up and close to wild boards, bears, and elephants who all come out to find water in the multiple drinking holes around the park.

3 Safari Drive in the **Masai Mara**

You may have read about the wildebeest migration in the first section of this book. In general, the Masai Mara is a classic safari destination and one of the best places to see lions, cheetahs, and leopards. Multiple tour companies offer safaris depending on individual traveler needs. You can book over three or even six days, a private or shared tour, and in a lodge or a tent. The best time of year to visit the Masai Mara is July to October, so no matter how you decide to go there, you will come away with very special memories.

4 Visit **Walruses** in Alaska

Located around seven small islands and their waters in the northern Bristol Bay, you can visit walruses in Alaska during the summer months. The Walrus Islands State Game Sanctuary protects them, and they also help with the protection of other habitats for types of seabirds and sea lions.

If you are considering visiting Alaska to experience other wildlife encounters, you may be interested in checking out the walruses as well. This is a remote wilderness experience and the best months to visit are May to mid-July.

5 Wildlife in
Galapagos

There technically isn't a 'wrong' time of year to experience wildlife in the Galapagos, but different times of the year have different things to see and do.

It's important to note that the Galapagos Islands are located in both the northern and southern hemispheres, but January, is the best time to see and experience green turtles as that's when they start laying their eggs. During this time, you will also see different varieties of iguanas with the land animals beginning their breeding season. From February to April, this is the breeding season for many of the mammals and birds that you will find there; therefore, this could be considered a prime time to go and experience the rich beauty and diversity that exists there.

6 Wildlife in Costa Rica

Costa Rica is only 10 degrees north of the equator. Thus, it doesn't really have seasons. If you have always imagined beautiful, unique wildlife in lush, colorful surroundings, then Costa Rica may be a great place for your travels! In particular, you could consider visiting the Monteverde Cloud Forest Reserve.

Here, you can experience different species of birds, frogs, and snakes and one of the biggest attractions is to look for uniquely colored quetzals. It is a renowned paradise for wildlife due to the diversity of animals that call it home.

TOP **6** WATER WILDLIFE ENCOUNTERS

1 Diving with
Tiger Sharks

You may be reading this section because you have already read about diving with tiger sharks in the section of this book titled "Top 9 Most Exciting Wildlife Encounters." There are a few places in the world which offer the chance to dive and see these creatures, including the Bahamas, Maldives, and Fiji.

In the Bahamas, there are several operators offering tours to go diving with tiger sharks, these are: Epic Diving, Stuart Cove and Reef Oasis Dive Club. They offer different diving packages and in general, there's a good chance that you will see up to species of shark at Tiger Beach. In the Maldives, Fuvahmulah Diving school offers tours to see and experience tiger sharks. We offer this one because Fuvahmulah is a unique island that is a rock in the middle of the open ocean at the Equator meaning that it is surrounded by many sharks and pelagic creatures. In Fiji, there are Coral Coast Divers, Bikini Bottom and Aqua Trek. You won't be disappointed as all offer beautiful dives across stunning coral reefs where you will discover all kinds of marine life.

2 Snorkel with **Manatees** and **Dugongs**

You may be reading this section because you have already read about diving with tiger sharks in the section of this book titled "Top 9 Most Exciting Wildlife Encounters."

There are several places in the world that offer the chance to snorkel with these creatures.

Crystal River in Florida is the only place in the US where you can do so and is also the place that boasts the largest concentration of them in the world. There are several tour guides and operators that offer packages, whether you want to do it in a group or on your own, there is something available for everyone.

3 Boating with **Whales** and **dolphins**

You may be reading this section because you have already read about diving with tiger sharks in the section of this book titled "Top 9 Most Exciting Wildlife Encounters." There are different parts of the world that offer this opportunity to boat with whales and dolphins, one, in particular, is French Polynesia.

For instance: the Inertia Network
Expeditions offer the possibility to
experience whales, and even swim with
them if desired. Not only that but also,
the program allows visitors to immerse
themselves within Polynesian culture as
a means of a connection between the
people, whales, and ocean.

4
Snorkeling
with Turtles

Many of us would love the chance to get up close and personal with turtles. These majestic, sweet animals can be seen alone gliding through the waters around the world. There are many spots where you can snorkel with turtles, one such example is around the Caribbean islands like Barbados. Multiple tour operators provide various packages for visitors to pay and enjoy experiences like snorkeling with turtles as well as other ocean marine life.

Islands in the Indian Ocean, such as the Maldives as well as Hawaii in the Pacific Ocean are great spots for turtle enthusiasts. If you are interested, hatching season is across the whole year, but usually in the summer months.

5 Diving in Baja California Sur

Diving in Baja California Sur is an unmissable opportunity for any diver who would love to discover beautiful marine life. It's possible to see Pacific manta rays around the waters of the La Reine dive site usually around June to October as well as sea lions frolicking in the water all year around!

There are many brilliant dive sites along the miles of water that stretches down the Baja California coast, including El Vencedor, and Cabo Pulmo National Marine Park which is on the East side of the peninsula. Here, you should see schooling jacks as well as the occasional bull shark.

6
Diving with
Whale Sharks

Whale Sharks are the largest known fish species that are found in open waters of tropical oceans.

There are several spots around the world where you can find them, including Baja California, Maledive, and Ningaloo Reef, Western Australia. You can book with multiple tour operators, including those that take a whole day to not only dive with whale sharks, but also explore the turquoise waters of the Ningaloo Reef to find many types of marine life. Read more in our extensive guide here.

SUMMARY

We hope you have enjoyed reading the book and finding the sections that you are most interested in. There are many more spectacular wildlife destinations in our world and other incredible wildlife experiences to have that haven't been included in this book, but we hope that the ones that we have included have inspired you to dream beyond your wildest imagination.

We live on a beautiful planet with a huge variety of biodiversity and wildlife, from swimming with orcas and whale sharks to driving a snowmobile through the snow and ice of Yellowstone past bison and elk herds. It's truly mind-blowing that all of this exists on our planet. If you want to know more about particular experiences or animals or are genuinely curious to learn more about wildlife, please visit www.animalsaroundtheglobe.com. If you have any questions about the content or what we have written about, please reach out to Feedback@animalsaroundtheglobe.com.

www.ingramcontent.com/pod-product-compliance
Lightning Source LLC
Chambersburg PA
CBHW081832250726
48662CB00020B/2554